The English Master of Defence

6 ᴴ5 ᵉ. 2.

THE

English MASTER of Defence:

O R,

The Gentleman's Al-a-mode Accomplishment

CONTAINING

The true Art of Single-Rapier or Small-Sword,
withal the curious Parres, and many more than the
vulgar Terms of Art plainly expreft, with the Names
of every particular Pafs, and the true performance
thereof, withal the exquifite Ways of Difarming and
Enclofing

AND

All the Guards at Broad-Sword and Quarter-
Staff, perfectly demonftrated, fhewing how the Blows,
Strokes, Chops, Thro s, Flirts, Slips and Darts, are
perform'd, with the true Method of Travefing.

ALSO

The exact Rules of Wreftling, explaining all the
nice Holds, both Out and In Catches, Hugs, Trips
and Locks, after what manner they are Taken, and
how to be Broken   The like was never Publifh't before by Man in *England,* but

By ZACH. WYLDE.

TORK·

Printed by *John White,* for the Author, 1711.

Mr. W. Marshall

... presenting to ye Shads this Speech ... ... fully assured yt ye ... was never so ptantly Exerted before by any Man, Which in my Glass ... ... Friends particular Re... ... ... a Gentleman of y Worth ... ... Address o more but I sincerely ... ... Great God ... Sovereign Moderator of all ... ... Ladies ...

Yr most humble Servant
is command ———

... Walle ———

TO THE
READER.

PRefaces, I confess, are become so common to every little Treatise, that I wonder there is not one to the Horn-Book; and indeed, oftentimes like Womens Faces, are found the most promising and inviting Part of the whole Piece: But when a thing is usual, tho' never so Ridiculous in the Eye of Reason, yet a Man (like him that spoils his Stomach with a Mess of Porridge before Dinner) may plead Custom to excuse his Error. I therefore hope it will be no Offence to conform with others, and show my self a Fool in Fashion.

Some Authors are such Fantastical Beaus in Writing, that they dress up each maggoty Fly-flirt, that creeps from their mouldy Fancy, with a fine Dedication, and a long Preface to a little Matter; like an Alderman's Grace to a Schollar's Commons; thinking their Pigmy Products looks as Naked without these Ornaments, as a Puritane without his Band, or a Whore without her Patches.

For my part, I only use this Preamble, as a Sow-Gelder does his Horn, that as by hearing of the latter, you may give a shrewd guess at his Business, so by reading of the former, you may rightly understand my design. Which is only to declare and publish what Experience I have gain'd in the Art of Small-Sword, Broad-Sword, Quarter-Staff, and Wrestling.

Whereas I'm at the Cost and Charge my self of Printing this ⌐*, upon Consideration, I have quite alter'd my measures and design in Publishing it to the view of all, only have such a Number printed, as I shall think will be suitable to my Purpose; by which means, I shall cut of the great Gain and Advantage the jugling Stationers would reap by it, and transfer it to my self. Now in this Case, all Men of Art and Learning, are highly obliged to our Magnanimous and Wise Parliament, in taking Cognizance of the grand Shams, Cheats, Tricks, and Abuses has*

been

To the READER.

been put upon *Authors* by *knavish* Printers Therefore their great *diserning* Eyes in *Judicature*, has thought fit to make an *Act* to *correct* such *Injuries* done to the *Propriators*, and confine 'em with-in the Bounds of *Justice*, with a great *Penalty* for every Offence committed.

I have omitted *Cuts* of the *Postures*, because several *Books* of this kind hath done it before, tho' in my Opinion, to little or no *Purpose*; for where I give an *Explanation* of the *Postures*, I think it is sufficient to satisfie the Curiosity of any one, and to save an unnecessary Expence. If this *Parvo*, which I Publish, meet with a free Acceptance from such worthy Gentlemen, as I presume to give the Dedication to, (whom I'm assured are most competent *Judges* of all *Difficulties* that lies in this Nature) I shall not in the least be concern'd what others will say about it, nor value the Censure of any carping, scurvy, scurrilous *Critick*.

Every Art and Science has it peculiar Terms, which are ob-scure to all who are not vers'd in 'em: Here you will find insert-ed several Terms of Art, that was never Publish't before, which are very necessary and material to the design, and proper to be known, which without 'em, it becomes but a confused *Notion* of *something* done or *acted*, without any distinct judicious *Knowledge* of the Method But I have taken such Care, as to clear all those *Difficulties* that may arise from such Terms of Art, as are not commonly known; for here they are all explain'd, not in obscure Words, but in such a plain familiar Method, as may render them easie to all Capacities

Rapier or Small-Sword, which is the first Subject I design to treat on. We find it according to some *Historians*, has its *Origi-nal* from the proud Spaniards, stately Italians, modish French, or truly I know not who, however we borrow it from some *Forreign* Place or other. And now 'tis become so common, that I suppose it is practised throughout *Christendom*, all *Nations* making such a wonderful improvement of the Art, that I believe 'tis grown near to Perfection (if a Man may so express it) especially in the Me-tropolis of this Kingdom Back or Broad-Sword, is a true Eng-lish *Weapon*, and first made use of in this Nation, so is Quarter-Staff, and likewise Wrestling, all which being highly necessary and convenient to be Understood, I need not speak in their Com-mendations, for their Merits will give 'em Praise enough

The

THE
English MASTER of Defence :

O R,

The Gentleman's Al-a-mode Accomplishment, &c.

Othing can give a greater Lusture and En-
noblement to the most Excellent and
Bravest Persons, than an absolute and
perfect Qualification in the true Knowledge and Skill in Weapons : In order to which, for
Gentlemens further Accomplishment, I Publish this
Book, which declares the whole secret of **Art**, con-
tain'd in Small-Sword, Broad-Sword, Quarter-Staff,
and Wrestling, &c.

'Tis altogether improper, neither *is* it consistent
with my Design in these Affairs, to make a long
Harangue of Discourse, to embroider and set off this
small Treatise, but immediately come home to my
intended Purpose. Therefore, I shall consume no
more time, but give the Reader, the Dimension,
Definition, or Division of a Small-Sword, Rapier or
Foil . In order thereunto, I will begin with the Hilt,
which I divide into Three Parts, thus nominated.
1*st*. The Pummel or end of the Hilt. 2*ly.* The
Handle or Middle. 3*ly*. The Shell or Front. The
Blade, I likewise divide into Three Parts thus, From
the Shell to the middle, I call the Fort or Strength
of the Weapon: The middle is the equal Part betwixt the Shell and the Point. From the middle to
the end, I call the Feeble or Weak.

Thus

THUS having given the Definition of a Small-Sword, before I nominate the Terms, by way of Caution, I shall declare to the Reader, Nine principal Observations, which ought continually to be kept in Memory, being the chief Rudiments and Grounds of the Art mentioned, as followeth, (*viz.*) Posture, Place, Compass, Step, Time, Distance, Patience, Intention, and Practice.

Imprimis, I shall begin with the Posture, thus demonstrated, Stand upon a true half Body, or edge wise, which I call, lie narrow your leading or right Foot, two Foot or more distant from the left, being in a direct Line from the same, then your right and left Foot will resemble a Roman Ⅴ; your Hand fast gript about the handle of your Foil or Rapier, then put your Thumb long ways or forward upon it, your Arm quite extended from the Center of your Body, the Point of the Weapon being directed in a true Line against your Opponent's right Pap, finking somewhat low with your Body, your right Knee bowing or bent over the Toes of your right Foot, (tho' some Masters teaches a strait Knee,) your left Knee more bent, inclining towards the Toes of your left Foot, lying in this Order is the Posture, which I call, Stand your Line, the Medium Guard then is fixt.

2*ly* Place is thus explain'd, When you stand your Line or Order as aforesaid, besure you observe never to alter your Arm from its Place; that is, from the Center of your Body, (tho' your Opponent uses all means to make you,) if you do, you certainly open and expose your self to his Advantage.

3*ly*. Compass may be taken in two Sences, that is, Compass in Defence, which is call'd the Parre, and Compass in Offence: Compass in Defence or the Pair.

Parre I define thus, When a Man Thrufts or Paffes at you, the Point of your Weapon fhou'd move about four Inches crofs ways from the Line, the Motion perform'd by the Wrift, your Arm kept in its certain Place, this Compafs will affuredly Parreor Defend you: Compafs in Offence or Offending, is thus, Never make or perform any Pafs or Thruft, but within the Killing part; if you fall your Point in a Thruft, you lofe a great Meafure of your Length, befides you extreamly hazzard your felf.

4*ly.* Step is no more than when you fhoot your felf extendedly, or to your full ftretch or length, which I call your Lônge

5*ly.* Time is taken in two Sences or two Ways, that if a Man Affaults at you, you muft not Thruft at the fame Juncture, if you do, you Counter-Tang, break Time and hazzard your felf: Otherwife, when you perceive a Man lies open, you may by the Quicknefs of your Thruft hit him before he Parre's you, which is falling within Time: Or when a Man finks his Arm in making of a Feint, especial-ly if he makes his Feint wide, you may eafily fall within Time.

6*ly.* Diftance is thus explain'd, You muft ftand fuch a Meafure or Diftance from the Party you are engaged with, as when you perform your Lônge, you can reach his Body to do Execution: Or thus, Admit your Weapons be upon equal length, if the Point of your's reach the Shell of your Opponents, you are then within Diftance.

7*ly.* Patience is defined thus, Let not Paffion, Fury, nor Choler, which are abfolute Enemies to skill, in no Cafe prevail, if you do, 'twill deftroy your Judgment.

8*ly.* Intention is to embrace an Opportunity when it prefents, by making Remarks where your Oppo-
Fittally.

nent lies moſt open; or by feigning a Thruſt to make him expoſe, then perform your Intention.

Finally, Practice is the Marrow and Quinteſſence of the Art, for without that, a Papiſt may ſoon forget his *Pater-noſter ;* but by frequent Practice, a Man gains much experience daily, and is continually improving his Skill. This being the laſt Obſervation, and one of the chief, no Opportunities of Practiſing ought to be neglected.

THUS having given a Caution, to keep in Memory theſe Obſervations : In the next Place, I ſhall define what I mean by a Parrœ, which *Note,* That which is call'd a Guard or Defence at Broad-Sword, is the ſame and equivolent to a Parr at Small-Sword, Broad and Small-Sword hath a certain dependance one upon another, in refference to the Guard, Parr or Defence, but not in the manner of Offence. For at Broad-Sword, all the Blows, Chops, Strokes, Pitches, Thro's, Flirts and Slips, are perform'd over the Point of the Sword, unleſs you fall to the Leg : But at Small-Sword, all Thruſts, Paſſes, Puſhes, Aſſaults, Eſſays and Paſſages, are commonly made under the Shell, (unleſs it be Cart or Ters over Arm,) cloſe to the Fort of your Opponents Weapon, with a Lónge, or you cannot reach to do Execution.

1ſt. The Parre or Parrade at Small-Sword, is perform'd thus, Stand your Line as directed, and if your Opponent makes an Aſſault or Thruſt at you, wave or move your Weapons point croſs-wiſe, the Compaſs of four Inch, from the Line downward and upward, according as the nature of the Paſs is made and ſo requires ; this Motion is perform'd by the Wriſt, about the Center of your Weapon, your Arm kept in its certain Place ; this I call the common Croſs way of Parring, and is the ſtrongeſt Parre

that

that can be made. Obferve that you make a Parre againft every pretended Thruft, for no Man knows anothers Intention, or whether he defigns to make his Pafs true or falfe.

2*ly.* If your Opponent makes a Ters thruft at you, you may Parr'it with the fame Edge you do Cart, and is fo taught by moft Mafters: howeyer I don't in the leaft approve on't, becaufe you give a great light to your Body; if your Opponent fhou'd happen to Feint upon you; in my Opinion, the other way is much the better, and far the quicker.

3*ly.* Another way of Parring, I call, The Orbicular Circular, or round Way or Manner, which is thus, Keep your Arm firm in its Place, as before directed, and if your Opponent difcharge, or prefents a Thruft at you, follow his Weapon round, by that means you may engage him continually. As for Example, If his Weapon engage or lie the infide your's, and if he makes a Pafs at you, either true or falfe, then turn your Point Circularly outward. If he engage or lie the outfide your Weapon, and Paffes at you, then turn your Point Circularly inward; thefe two Ways, Pairés all Paffes true or falfly made, if rightly timed.

4*ly.* You may Parré two Ways more Circularly, by a different way of lying; that is, dipping your Point near the Ground, half a Yard wide the infide your Opponent's right Foot, then if he Paffes at you, recover towards the infide, which will meet engage his Weapon, and compleat a Parre. If you lay your Point wide on the outfide his Foot when he Paffes at you, then recover towards the outfide, which will make an abfolute Parre, If you lie in either of thefe Ways or Order, a Man can't Feint upon you; for no Man can Feint, unlefs you lie in a Line fomewhat advanc't with your Weapon.

B

5*ly.* An-

5*ly.* Another way of Parring, I call, The Semi-
Circular, or half Moon Parry, which is thus, Lie in
your Order, according to your firſt Direction, in a
true Line; then lower or dip the Point of your Weapon about two Inch, lying the inſide your Opponent's; then if he Thruſts at you, make a half Circle,
which will meet his Thruſt, and Parr him. If you
lie with your Weapon's Point the outſide his, in like
manner as aforeſaid, and he Thruſts at you, return
your Weapon into its firſt Place, and you'l reingage
him with the Blade of your Weapon, and perfect
a Parræ. This Parre is the moſt abſolute and com-
pleateſt Parræ that ever was invented, and without
Oſtentation, I can truly ſay, I was the firſt Perſon
that Taught it; and I dare further affirm, that
there's many Proffeſſors of this Noble Art, that
knows no more of the half Moon Parry, than they
do of the Man in the Moon.

6*ly.* Another different Way of Parring, is thus,
Stand upon a full Body, and extend your Sword
Arm ſtrait from you; then turn your Wriſt Ters-
wiſe, and dip or hang the Point of your Weapon,
but obſerve to ſee your Oppnent's Head under the
Hilt of it, then if he Thruſts to your open, engage
upon him with the Blade of your Weapon, which
makes a full Parræ; but if he ſhou'd make a ſecond
Aſſault in Ters, return your Weapon into its Place
from whence it came, and 'twill reingage him and
Parr his Thruſt; this I call, The Falloon Poſture
with its Parræ.

7*ly.* Another way of Parring, I call Palming,
thus demonſtrated, Stand your direct Line as aforeſaid, and lie with your Weapon full Ters, hold
your left Hand in manner of a half Moon annenſt
your Chin, or Clap the back of it upon your right
Pap; then if your Opponent Puſhes at you, inſtead

of

of Parring with your Sword, Palm with your left Hand, and quicker than I can speak, perform your Pass in Cart.

8*ly*. Lie fully guarded in Cart, and when your Opponent pushes at you in Ters, Palm, and make a return of your Thrust in Cart.

9*ly*. Lie in Falloon Posture, and when your Opponent assaults at you, Palm with your left Hand, and immediately return your thrust Cart-ways.

10*ly*. You may drop or descend your Point near the Ground; then you give a clear open to your Body, and when your Opponent makes his Pass at you, Palm, and answer in a direct Line.

11*ly*. Otherways, you may stand upon a true half Body, with your left Foot foremost; then extend your left Arm out strait from you, and lay the Point of your Sword upon the Back of your left Hand, but discover your Opponent's Head under your left Arm; then if he Passes at you, Palm, and immediately step forward with your right Foot, and put in your Pass with the greatest Celerity imaginable, in a direct Line. Thus much as to Parring and Palming.

THE next thing I shall proceed to, is to the Terms of Art and Variety of Assaults, Pushes, Thrusts, Essays, Passes and Passages, all which are lodged under the Notion of True and False Play. True Play is a clean made Pass, Push, Assault or Thrust, directly perform'd, without change or alteration of the Point of your Weapon at any part or place of your Opponent you discover lies most open, or in answering your Opponent from his Assault. False Play or Falsifying, I call Quibles, Dazzels, Feints, Fallacies, Shams, Decoi's and Enganuo's, all which I shall explain in their Order.

There-

Therefore I shall begin with the two fundamental, supream, and head Terms of Art, Cart and Ters, from whence all other Springs has their Origin and Derivation. Tho' *Note*, That I can but thrusts Cart and Ters, or Cart in Ters place properly ; yet notwithstanding, in change and course of Play, Springs variety of other Terms, that I give Names to according as the Assaults, Passes and Thrusts are perform'd. Take notice, That the only Observation, Experience teaches me in reference, to know or apprehend how a Man pushes at you, whether it be in Cart or in Ters, is to fix your Eye, not upon his Eye, which is a vulgar Error, but upon the Shell of his Weapon ; for by making a diligent Remark there, 'twill plainly discover to you the Intent and Purport of any Man's Push or Assault.

Imprimis, Cart is perform'd thus, Stand your Line as aforesaid, and let all the Weight of your Body depend upon the left Foot ; then present your Pass the inside your Opponents Weapon, as near as possible you can to the Fort of it, your Finger Nails looking upwards, your Blade then will be Flat, with a *Stiff* extended Arm, timing your step with the Motion of your Body forward, shooting your self to your full stretch or length ; and upon terminating your Thrust, your Face ought to lie as low as the Hilt of your Rapier, which is the only safety in your Thrust ; but keep the inside of your left Foot fast on the Ground like an Anchor, to pluck home your Body and right Foot into their Place and Distance again, this is call'd your Longein Cart.

2ly. Ters is perform'd contrary to Cart, for it's pusht over the right Arm, the outside your Opponents Weapon, your Wrist turn'd outward almost round from you, (then your Finger Nails looks downward,) with a stiff Arm.

The

The moſt abſolute and trueſt way of thruſting Cart and Ters, is to perform your Paſs as cloſe to the Fort of your Opponents Weapon as you can; for in ſo doing, it will in a great Meaſure preſerve you, if he happen to Counter Tang: but if your Puſh fails hitting, beſure to make your recovery ſtrongly engaged upon his Weapon, or ſpring your ſelf backward withal the Celerity imaginable out of his diſtance, in a true Line; I call this Revoltier, or a Retrograde from an Aſſault.

Note, That you may puſh Cart in Ters with ſafety, but not Ters in Carts place; if you do, you certainly expoſe your ſelf in the performance of your Thruſt: I deny making any Anſwer with your Wriſt turn'd Ters, (tho' its taught by moſt Profeſſors, eſpecially in the Performance of a Sacoon; but I'll vindicate it to be a grand Error, before the beſt Maſter in Chriſtendom, and I do affirm that Ters ought not to be thruſt, but ſingle in its own Place,) unleſs it be a Sequence in Ters; never Feint it, by reaſon you loſe ſo much time in turning your Wriſt.

3ly. A Reſponſe or Anſwer, is made or perform'd when a Man puſhes to you in Cart; then Parr and return in like manner, with the greateſt Celerity that can be.

4ly. A Flancanade paſs, is perform'd when a Man puſhes to you in Cart, then Parr'and Anſwer Cartways engaging, or locking his Weapon as you finiſh your Paſs.

5ly. A Reverſe is made, when a Man puſhes to you in Cart, Parr and bring your Point round his Shell, and conclude your Paſs Cart in Ters a Gee.

6ly. A Paſſage is a clean ſwift Thruſt, put in like a Dart, either in Cart or Ters.

7ly. A Sequence in Ters, is made when a Man Puſhes in Ters, Parr'and Anſwer ſtrongly engaged in Ters.

8ly. A

8ly. A Second or Sacoon direct is made, when a Man Pushes to you in Ters, or Cart in Ters; then Parr'and shoot in your Pass Cartways under his Arm-pit.

9ly. A Counter Caveating Thrust, is made thus, Engage the Center of your Opponents Weapon in Cart; then perform your Pass fully engaged, or locking his Weapon as you terminate your Thrust, there is but a little difference betwixt this and a Flan-canade; only this is made Volunteer, and the other upon an Answer.

10ly. You may perform the like Thrust by engag-ing the Feeble of your Opponents Weapon in Ters, then shoot your Pass in entirely engaged, there can be no better or safer Thrust made, than either of these to an ignorant Person, for your engaging of him Prevents his breaking Time, and thrusting with you: (But this I declare, there's no Man living can promise a safety in his Thrust, if his Opponent Counter Tangs, that is, Pushes at the same juncture, its not in the Power of Art to elude, but you may both be hit.) You may perform either of these a-bove specified Passes upon a Responie or Answer to any Man.

11ly. A Mountanto, is perform'd by laying the Point of your Weapon on the Ground, sinking very low with your Body; and when your Opponent Pushes at you by a sudden spring, raise your self in-to a good Posture, strike up his Weapon in the Parry to make you a free Passage, and conclude your Pass in order of a Sacoon.

12ly. A clear free Flancanade or low Cart, is made when your Opponent lies advanc't with his Wea-pon, then shoot your Pass in, in a direct Line, quick as an Arrow out of a Bow Cartways, to the Bottom of the Belly.

13ly. A

13*ly*. A Stockata, is made thus, Lean back with your Body, and by a sudden shoot, put in your Pass in Cart, or you may Coopee, which is Reversing, and 'twill prove a Cheating thrust.

14*ly*. A Falloon, is thus made, Stand upon a full Body, and extend your Arm out Ters way, dipping or hanging the Point of your Weapon, but observe to see your Opponent's Head under the Hilt of your Rapier; then if he Passes at you, Parr and Answer in Cart or Coopee.

15*ly*. A Battery, is made thus, Strike or Batter on the inside your Opponent's Weapon, and Push from the Battery quick as Lightning in Cart or Coopee. 16*ly*. So to the contrary, Batter on the outside a Man's Weapon, and push Sacoonways.

17*ly*. A Roul, is made thus, Twist or turn your Weapon round, by the Motion of your Wrist Cartways, then Push in Teis. 18*ly*. Roul in Teis and Push in Cart. 19*ly*. Engage strongly in Cart, and Push from Engagement or Coopee. 20*ly*. Engage likewise in Teis, and Push Sacoonways.

Note, That every Pais, Push, Assault, or Thrust you make, be in a direct Line, (which I call true Planting of a Thrust) with a stiff extended Arm, and in the same Posture make your Recovery. So much as to True Play, or single or plain Thrusting.

Take notice, That if I join Touch, Engage, Embogue, Stringer, Bind, Caveat, or Rely upon your Weapon, 'tis all one and the same thing; but in all Cases observe, That if you do Engage, or Caveat a Man's Weapon, let it be with the greatest Ease imaginable, then you may with freedom Disengage.

That nothing might seem obscure to the Eye of Reason, in this small Volum, I think it may be proper to give and explain a Methodical Lesson, which compendiously Sums up the Heads of all the Terms

of

of Art, and the Performances of Assaults and Re-
nisths, according to the Rule of True Play.

Imprimis, Stand your Line as directed, and Lie in
Cart, then Assault in Ters. 2*ly.* Lie in Ters, and
Assault in Cart. 3*ly.* Lie in Cart, and Push low Cart.
4*ly.* Lie in Ters, and Push full in Ters. 5*ly.* Lie in
Cart of Coopee, Cart in Ters a Gee, or Cart over
Shell. 6*ly.* Batter in Cart, and Push in Cart. 7*ly.*
Batter in Cart and Coopee. 8*ly.* Batter in Ters,
and Push Sacoonways. 9*ly.* Engage in Cart, and
Push from Engagement or Coopee. 10*ly.* Engage in
Ters, and Push Sacoonways. 11*ly.* Lie engaged
Tersways in Ters place, and shoot your Cart in with
great Celerity. 12*ly.* Lie engaged Cart in Ters, and
wheel in your Ters. 13*ly.* Roul in Cart, and Push
in Ters. 14*ly.* Roul in Ters, and Push in Cart.
(thus much for single Assaulting.) 15*ly.* If your
Opponent Pushes to you in Cart, Parre and Answer
Flancanadeways. 16*ly.* If he thrusts again in Cart,
Parre and make a Response. 17*ly.* If he thrusts a
third time in Cart, Parre and Reverse, or Coopee.
18*ly.* If he thrusts a fourth time in Cart, thrust Flan-
canade at the same juncture. 19*ly.* If he thrusts a
fifth time in Cart, make an half Moon Parre, and
return your thrust, I call this cutting a Cart; which,
I'll assure you, is a great Master-piece of Art; and
I do positively Affirm, I was the first Man that
taught it. 20*ly.* If your Opponent Assaults a sixth
time in Cart, make a Falloon Parre, and return your
Thrust or Coopee. 21*st.* If your Opponent Assaults
in Ters at you, Parre and Answer strongly engaged
in Ters, which is commonly call'd a Sequence. 22*ly.*
If he Assaults again in Ters, Parre and Push in the
Sacoon. 23*ly.* If he Assaults a third time in Ters,
thrust Ters at the same time you have lockt his Wea
pon, for your Security. Observe, That you may
make

make the fame Returns from the Circular Parre, as you do from the Crofs; which truly perform'd, your Opponent will find it a difficult thing to efcape from being hit by fuch Returns. 24*ly.* If your Opponent Affaults you at any time with a Cart thruft, Parre, then feize the Feeble of his Weapon, with your left Hand, and Anfwer in a direct Line. 25*ly.* If he thrufts to you in Ters, Parre, then ftep in with your left Foot, feize the Fort of his Weapon, and with draw your's, or Plant a thruft upon him. 26*ly.* Make a full and home thruft to your Opponent in Cart, and at the fame time as he Parre's, ftep into an enclofure, and feize his Weapon, then ufe your Difcretion. 27*ly.* Thruft full in Ters, and as foon as he Parres, enclofe, and perform as aforefaid. 28*ly.* Engage your Opponents Weapon in Cart, then enclofe, by feizing the Feeble of his Weapon, with your left Hand; fo you'l have him at your Mercy. 29*ly.* Engage your Opponents Weapon in Ters, then feize the Fort of his Weapon, with your left Hand; enclofe, and perform as aforefaid. 30*ly.* Lie lofe or difengage in Ters, then engage in Cart, and enclofe. 31*ft.* Lie difengaged in Cart, then engage in Ters, and enclofe and perform as aforefaid. You may eafily enclofe upon any Engagement, either in Cart or Ters; but lying lofe is more furprizing to your Adverfary.

T H E next thing that I fhall explain, is Falfe Play, Feinting or Falfifying; which is perform'd from Engagement, or clearly quitted or difengaged.

1*ft,* A Falfifying Pafs, is made by a quick change of the Point of your Weapon, in and outfide your Opponent's, as thus, Engage or join Weapon on the infide his, then pretend to Pufh or Thruft in Ters, and finifh in Cart, this I call a fingle Feint or Falfify.

C   2*ly.* En-

2*ly.* Engage in Teis, and pretend in Cait, then conclude in Ters, is another fingle Feint. 3*ly.* You may perform thefe two different Ways of Feinting, when your Weapons is free from Engagement. 4*ly.* Another Feint is made by Battering the infide a Man's Weapon, and Feint from the Battery. 5*ly.* Batter on the outfide a Man's Weapon, and Feint from the Battery. 6*ly.* Engage ftrongly in Cart, and Feint. 7*ly.* Engage likewife in Teis, and Feint. 8*ly.* A Feint-Semi, is made thus, Let your firft Pretence be in Ters, then in Cart, fo end in Ters. 9*ly.* Otherwife, pretend in Cart, then in Ters, and finifh in Cait. 10*ly.* A Fine Pafs is no more than a Treble change of your Weapon. 11*ly.* A Super-Fine Pafs, is made by multiplying, or feveral times changing your Point in and outfide the Fort of your Opponent's Weapon, to diforder his Part, and fo perform'd according as you find him expos'd. 12*ly.* A Feintelæteight, is no more than a treble Fallacy or Feint. 13*ly.* An Imbrocata, is the fame as Superfine Pafs. 14*ly.* A Roul feinted in a different manner, is a grand furprizing Cheat. 15*ly.* A Counterchange, is made thus, Stand upon a ftretch, or extendedly with your Legs, then draw your left Foot up to the right, and terminate your Longewith a Feint; this may be done in different manner, *viz.* Firft perform'd in Cart, then in Ters. 16*ly.* A Falfe Battery is made, by Battering the infide a Man's Weapon, then Feint from your Battery. 17*ly.* Batter on the outfide your Opponent's Weapon, from whence you Feint. 18*ly.* A Super-fine Tozure, is perform'd by turning or wheeling the Point of your Weapon feveral times round your Opponents, then vary it two or three times, and finifh in Cait or Teis 19*ly.* A Fallacy from a double Engagement, is made thus, Engage in Cait, then in Ters, and

make

make a single Feint. 20*ly.* Engage in Ters, then in Cart, from whence you Feint. 21*st.* A Ran' Counter, is made thus, Engage in Cart, then in Ters, and double your Feint. 22*ly.* An Enganuo, is made much a like to a Falsifying Pass or Feint, only made treble, in order to discompose your Opponent's Parts, then conclude in Cart or Ters. 23*ly.* A Catastraphoon, is Composed of a Falsifying, Quibling, Dazling, Feinting Pass, made Super-fine, or as oft as your Fancy directs, and finisht according as you find your Opponent expos'd. 24*ly.* A Feint Royal, is comprehended of the Excellency and Quintessence of Superfine Passes, most dexterously, accurately and vigorously perform'd, withal the Life, Vivacity, Quickness and Celerity, that can be imagined or exprest.

NOW I present to the Reader, an absolute and perfect Lesson, comprehending False Play, Feinting and Falsifying.

Imprimis. Posture your Body narrow, or in an exact Line, engage the Center of your Opponent's Weapon, with the feeble of your's in Cart, then Feint, single from Engagement. 2*ly.* Engage in Ters, with the Feeble of your Weapon, from whence you make a single Feint. 3*ly.* Lie in Cart clearly quitted or disengaged, then perform a single Feint. 4*ly.* Lie disengaged in Ters, and make a single Feint. 5*ly.* Batter in Cart and Feint. 6*ly.* Batter in Ters and Feint. 7*ly.* Engage strongly in Cart and Feint. 8*ly.* Engage likewise in Ters and Feint. 9*ly.* Roul in Cart and Feint. 10*ly.* Roul in Ters and Feint. 11*ly* Lie in Cart, and make a fine Pass, a Superfine Pass, or an Enganuo 12*ly* Lie in Ters, and perform the like. 13*ly* Lie in a Falloon Posture, and Feint. 14*ly.* Lie in Cart, and make a Counterchange. 15*ly.* Perform the like, by lying in Ters.

16*ly.* Make

16*ly.* Make a single Feint, from a double Engage-ment. 17*ly.* Make an Enganuo from a Roul. 18*ly.* Make a Super-fine Tozure from a Battery, or a Feint Royal. 19*ly.* If your Opponent Assaults upon you, Answer with a Feint, or a Fine Pass. 20*ly.* If he makes a second Assault, Palm, and make your An-swer quicker than I can speak. 21*ly.* If he Assaults again Disarm. All these Passes and Answers are to be perform'd, according to the Directions herein specified.

'Tis a grand Surprize, when a Man pushes in Cart to you, then Parre; but before you quit Engagement, seize the Feeble of his Weapon, with your left Hand, then perform your Pass, in a direct Line, quick as thought; if this be done with great Celeri-ty, 'tis much odds you may Push or hit any Man. Otherwise, If a Man makes a full Thrust in Ters at you, Parre, and at the same time step in with your left Foot, with all the Life and Quickness imagina-ble, seizing the Fort of his Weapon, with your left Hand; then you have him at your Mercy (I've given an hint of this in my first Lesson, but not so fully.) Some Gentlemen, that I've shew'd this Piece of Art, 'counts it not fair Play, but I'm not in the least of their Opinion : (my Reason is this) Admit that I have imprudently drawn my self into a Quarrel, then my Life lies at Stake; therefore, I think it no Point of Dishonour to assume all the Ad-vantage I can, in my own Defence, against my En-emy.

Take notice, That in Feinting or Falsifying, I wou'd advise never to exceed a treble, lest your Op-ponent shou'd break Time, and thrust with you, for in such a Case, you extreamly hazard : And further, Observe, That when you Feint, keep your Aim in its Place, don't fall it, if possible, an Hairs breadth;

if you do, you likewise hazard. A Close at Small-Sword is perform'd thus, Make a full Thrust in Cart, and at the same juncture, as your Opponent Paries, step in with your left Foot; withal Expedition, and with your left Hand seize his Weapon, hold it fast, and with draw yours so far back that the Point thereof reach but the Center of your Body, then use your most merciful Discretion. You may perform the like by thrusting full in Ters, and perform as aforesaid.

THE Way, Method, and Manner of Disarming, which is perform'd by engaging the Weapon, or encroaching upon your Opponent to an enclosure.

Imprimis, Engage in Cart, with the Fort of your Weapon upon the Center of your Opponents, then by a sudden spring or jerking Twist, force it towards his Elbow, so you may cast or thro' it out of his Hand You may perform the like, by engaging his Weapon in Ters in like manner, but its not so easily done as aforesaid. This I call a single lose Disarm.

2*ly.* If a Man pushes to you in Cart, Parry, and bind or engage firm upon his Weapon with yours; then with your left Hand make seizure of the Fort of his Blade near the Shell, so you'l have him upon a Lock; then by putting your right Arm from you, and by a sudden Twitch, pluck your left Hand to you, you may Disarm. You may perform this way of your own free Will, that is, join your Weapon on the inside your Opponents, and Disarm as aforesaid.

3*ly.* Make a full and home Thrust Cart in Ters, directly to your Opponent's Face, and as soon as he Parre's, rest upon Engagement; then step in with your left Foot, and with your left Hand, the back thereof being turn'd towards your Face, you may

seize

feize his Weapon; then by putting your right Hand
ftiffly up, and pull down your left, with the great-
eft Force and Quicknefs imaginable, fo Difarm.

4ly. Join your Weapon on the outfide your Opponent's, then wheel or turn round his with the Blade
of your's, and with your left Hand take hold of the
middle of his Blade, under your Arm, then twift
it out Backward.   This I call the wheeling Difarm,
which is a moft excellent way, if truly perform'd

5ly. Join or engage Flancanadeways in Cart, then
ftep in with your left Foot, and with your left Arm
in the bent of it, feize the Fort of his Weapon,
pluck your left Arm ftrongly to you, and put your
right Hand ftiffly from you, fo Difarm.

6ly. Join the edge of your Weapon againft the
flat of your Opponent's Center, then take hold upon his Fort, with your left Hand, force your right
Hand forward, and fuddenly pluck your left Hand
to you; fo with great facility, but withal ufe agil-
lity, you may Difarm.

Finally, Join your Cart edge on the middle of
your Opponent's Cart, prefs or poife his Weapon towards his Back, then clafp your left Hand upon the
Fort of it, a little above your's, pluck your left
Hand to you, and forceably put your right Hand
from you; fo if I be not miftaken, you may Difarm, &c.

---

*Rules and Directions to be obferv'd at Back or
Broad-Sword.*

IMprimis, The Guards in Number are Five, commonly call'd, dignified, or diftinguifh'd by the
Names of the Out-fide, Infide, Medium, Gorge,
or Hanging . Otherways call'd the Dexter, or right
Guard,

Guard, Sinifter or left Guard, Center Unicorn or Medium, Diamiter or Górge, Pendent or the Hanging Guard.   Having declared to the Reader the Names of the Guards, I'll begin with the Outfide or Dexter, thus demonftrated, Stand upon a true half Body, and extend your Sword-Hilt out at the Arms end ftiff, without bowing the Elbow-joint, your Point leaning or floping towards your left Shoulder, or your Oppofer's right Eye, lying as hollow as you can with your Body; then you may fee your Oppofer the infide your Swoid, fo long as you keep this Guard: You lying on this manner, if your Oppofer charge you with a Blow, Pitch, Stroke, Flirt, or Chop on the out or right Side, which is all one, you are then defended, or upon a fure Guard: But if ftrikes at your left Ear, or infide commonly call'd, then you muft prepare an infide or left Guard, which is to be made on this manner, Crofs the outfide Guard, that is, a little twift or turn your Wrift towards your left Shoulder, your Arm kept ftrait from you; then your Point will be floping towards your Oppofer's left Eye, and you may fee his Body the outfide your Sword, while you keep this Guard.   *Note,* That as you move your Sword either to the out or infide, carry your Point almoft ereĉt, but fomewhat a little floping, thefe two Guards will Guaid you fecurely, if rightly timed, fo long as you keep out at length. The Medium Unicoin or Center Guard, is made thus, Extend your Arm ftrait out at length, and your Sword placed betwixt your Oppofer's Eyes, lying true half Body, your Sword-Hilt as high as your Chin, keeping it out at the Arms end ftiff; then if he charge you with a Blow or Stroke either to the in or outfide, crofs his Swoid, which makes a perfeĉt Guard · This Guard keeps your Oppofer from encioaching upon you, if he does, he endangers himself. The Górge is seldom used, but when a down right Blow or Pitch is made at the Head, then prepare the Górge thus, Extend your Arm out stiff, and with your Sword cross your own or your Opposer's Forehead, then your Point will be level with the Hilt; but before that your Pitch be to that height, that you can see your Opposer's Head eight Inch under your Guard; I don't esteem this a good Guard to lie on, by reason I am exposed in two Places. The last is the Pendent or Hanging Guard, which is the surest and best Guard that can be made, a Man can't come up to half Sword, without this Guard, it's made on this manner, Extend your Arm stiffly out, and turn your Knuckles outward, then hold your Hilt half a Foot or more, higher than your Head, then the Point of your Weapon must slope or hang dipping towards the outside of your Opposer; but before you look just under the Hilt, and observe to see your Opposer's Head six or seven Inch under it continually, or else you cannot be safe: When you lie on this manner, you then will be exposed or lie open on the outside, which may be Guarded by pitching your Point to the outside of your Body, or coming to an outside Guard: I approve of this to be the best of Guards, especially if you meet with a Rustick, down right Striker, for it almost saves the whole Body; whereas any other Guard saves but half at one time. So much for Defence or Guards at Sword.

You may raise or thro' your Guards on this manner, Stand upon a full or entire Body, and ground your Sword Point at or upon the Toes of your right Foot, then advance your Arm, and bring the Point of your Sword by your left Ear, round the back-side of your Head, so by a little twist of the Wrist, you come to an inside Guard; but observe, That at the same juncture that you raise your Sword, step with right Foot half a Yard or more distant from the left, being in a direct Line from the middle of your left Foot, the Toes of your right Foot turn'd a little outwards, then you may see your Opposer's Body the outside your Sword: From thence you may come to an outside Guard thus, by returning your Sword the same way it came, likewise your Foot, and come to the Place of an outside: From your outside you may come to a Medium, by dropping your Point, and bring it by your left Ear, then place it betwixt your Opposer's Eyes: From thence you may come to a Gorge, by returning your Sword round the back of your Head, then come to the Place of a Gorge. From the Gorge cast or thro' your Point upon a Level from you, then by a great Compass round, you may come to the Hanging Guard, &c. To practise Raising or Thro'ing the Guards on this manner, you'l find 'em to be your true Grounds and Rudiements of Falsifying: Without boasting, I was the first Man that ever taught or shew'd the Method of Raising or Thro'ing the Guards.

Offence or Offending is perform'd thus, When your Opposer makes an inside Blow or Pitch at you, Guard him with an inside, and Pitch quick to his outside, which upon the fall of his Blow will be exposed. When he strikes to your outside, Chop quick to his open on the inside, according to the Rule of True Play; and in this Case, let all your Answers be made as quick as the Hand can perform 'em. If you Exercise with any Man, before you make your False Play, prove him with True Play, to know what Guards he'll make, then your False Play or Falsifying will happen better in their Order. 1*st.* Let your first Assault be a quarter Blow and half, or a quick Chop, perform'd by the Wrist, upon a

D Medium

Medium, directly to your Oppofer's Face, there you'l
apprehend whether he'l make an in fide Guard or no
But *Note,* That as foon as you have deliver'd either
Pitch, Blow, or Chop, befure to recover your Sword
into its Place again, left your Oppofer hit you before Recovery.

True Play is to Pitch or Strike at the Place you
fee lies moft open, whether it be in or outfide : So
that when you've proved your Oppofer with True
Play, then you may offer a feigned Pitch or Blow at
the Place you difcover lies open, and as he endeav-
ours to Guard his open, then Pitch your Blow or
Chop into the contrary. A Falfify is made fingle,
double, treble, quadruple, quintuple, or as oft as
your Fancy directs; for as you apprehend your Oppofer changes his Guard, change with him, and being more quick than he, you may Pitch into an open.
If you come to Engage with any Man, lie upon a
full outfide, and wade your Weapon in the Place
you lie in, by the Motion of the Wrift, but keep
your Arm in its Place, then Chop it home to his in
fide : fo perform the fame from an In to an Outfide.
From your wading upon out or infide, you may
make a Falfify fingle, *double* or treble; but befure you
don't alter your Aim, but keep it in its certain Place.

A Blow I call the Swoop, is made when you lie
upon an outfide thus, Let your Point drop Hanging-
wife, and bring it round the Point of your Opponent's Sword, and Pitch it home to his Face Or o-
therways, you may turn this Swoop into a Falfify,
by feinting to come on the infide, then change it
quick, and finifh your Stroke on the outfide. 'Tis a
grand Cheat to make a full Thruft to your Opponent's Face, the infide his Sword, and when his
Sword Anfwers or Guards your's, turn your Stroke
round over his Point to the right Ear or outfide So
to

to the contrary, Thruft to his Face the outfide his Sword, and conclude your Blow on the infide; 'tis a difficult thing to Guard either of thefe Aſſaults, if the Hand be quick that performs 'em. A fingle Falſify, is made by feigning or offering a Blow or Stroke on the infide, and conclude it on the outfide; or pretend to make a Blow on the out, and finifh upon the infide. Another Falfify, is made by feigning a Blow to the outfide of the Head, and immediately fall it to the infide of the right Leg, or pretend to Strike at his left Ear, then conclude upon the outfide of his right Leg; but before you confume no time in your Recovery. Likewife, you may offer a Blow at the infide of the Leg, and turn it over to the outfide of the Head: Another deluding Cheat at Sword, is made thus, Lie upon a Medium, then turn to the Hanging, but at the fame juncture approach or encroach one Step, then finifh with a fingle Falfify. Another grand Deceit, is to make a Falfify with a Step, which you make in different manner, that is, lie upon an outfide Guard and inſide Step, then offer a Blow with your Step to the in, but end it on the outfide: fo pretend to Strike with your Step to the out, then conclude it on the infide.

The chiefeft Rule you are to obferve at Sword, is firft your True Play as aforefaid; the next in courfe of Play, have a fpecial regard to a Slip, thus explain'd, Lie as hollow as you can, with your Body upon a full outfide, then if your Opponent Pitches or Thro's to your infide, by a quick Spring, or fudden Advance of your Arm, quite out of his reach, being exactly timed as he delivers his Pitch, he miſſing your Guard, the ftrength of his Blow will carry his Sword beyond diftance of Guard, fo that you may eafily hit him before Recovery; but let your Anfwer be Pitcht in directly upon a Medium, with-al

al the Life and Quickneſs imaginable. You may
ſlip from lying upon any Guard whatever, but beſure that you obſerve your Diſtance ; if you don't,
you may be hit in making of a ſlip ; then, in my O-
pinion, you'l make but a bad Piece of work on't :
Your Diſtance is, if the Point of your Sword reach
ten or twelve Inch over your Opponent's Hilt, you
may ſlip with ſafety ; or in making of a ſlip, you
may break Meaſure, by falling back with your Body. You may make a double Slip thus, When you Obſerve that your Opponent underſtands a Slip and
Slips, you then time it right, and Slip him ; I count
this the excellency of Play, which may be acquired *to*
by frequent Practice. Without vain Glory, I was
the firſt Perſon that ever Taught or Perform'd the
double Slip : (Tho' if one Man had the Excellency
of all Men, yet notwithſtanding, he would be neither
valued or eſteem'd in ſome Places, eſpecially amongſt
the Ignorant and Ignoble.) Obſerve, That when
you make either Blow, Pitch, Stroke or Chop,
True or Falſe, let 'em be perform'd as quick as the
Hand can thro' them in ; then recover upon the
Hanging Guard, which is your greateſt ſafety : Sup-
poſe that you be ſlipt juſt as you perceive that you
loſe your Point, turn your Wriſt to the Hanging,
which is in all Caſes the moſt abſolute and ſureſt
Guard or Defence.

Note, That your Play at Broad-Sword is different from Small-Sword, for Broad-Sword is plaid
Circularly, that is upon Traverſe, in which, if you
be cunning, you may pick ſeveral Advantages. *Ob-*
ſerve, That if your Opponent drops to your Leg, at
the ſame time ſlip your Leg back out of his reach,
then return your Stroke as ſpeedily as poſſible · If
you fall to the Leg, let it be by a Falſify, that is,
offer a Pitch to the outſide of his Head, or right Ear,

then

then fall to the infide of his Leg; this will concern
him fo much with his Guards, that you cannot
hazard.

A Clofe at Broad-Sword is perform'd thus, Engage
your Opponent's Sword on the infide withal your
Strength, then force it backward as low as his Knee,
and at the fame time ftep in with your left Foot,
and feize the Feeble of his Blade with your left Hand,
then execute your Intention: You may perform the
like by engaging on the outfide his Sword, and perform as aforefaid: You may Difarm either of thefe
Ways, after the fame manner as you do at Small-
Sword. Otherwife, Lie upon a low Guard, or rather no Guard; that is, hold your Sword as low as
your middle, fo that all the upper Part of your Body be bare, or clearly expofed; and when your Opponent ftrikes at your Head, Pitch to the hanging
Gard, and at the fame juncture ftep in with your
left Foot, and with your left Hand, the back thereof
being turn'd towards your Face, make feizure of his
Sword, then ufe your moft merciful Difcretion.
Take notice, That if your Opponent ftrikes at the
fame time as you do, I call it a Counter Tempt,
which be careful to avoid.

Ever fince I have Taught this noble Art of Fencing,
it has been my Obfervation, that many Gentlemen;
efpecially fome topping Mafters in their own Con-
ceits, that only teaches Small-Sword, will not in the
leaft allow one Man to underftand, or be an Artift in
three Sorts of Weapons, to wit, Small-Sword, Broad-
Sword & Quarter-Staff, (adding Wreftling,) thefe are
them that are the Subject of my Difcourfe: Truly,
I much wonder at their great Ignorance, for it may
be as well faid, that an Eminent and Excellent Phy-
fician, whofe univerfal Knowledge and Fame is extended through the whole Kingdom, knows but a
fingle

single Medicine, or can Prescribe but one way to
Cure a Distemper, (which doubtless has twenty.)
Or that a very Famous and Able Musician can but
Play or Teach of one Instrument; truly, in my O-
pinion, there is as much Reason for one as the o-
ther: Therefore I shall not in the least trouble my
self to undeceive their incredulity, &c. Whereas
I have made it plainly appear, that Small-Sword
and Broad-Sword, hath such a dependance one upon
another, in sundry Respects ought to be linckt together; for the Cross Parreat Small-Sword, is the
same and equivolent to the in and out Gard at Broad-
Sword. The Falloon Parr is the same as the Pendent
or Hanging Guard, there's no difference in the least,
as to the Ways of Parring and Guarding. Further,
give me leave to State a Case, Suppose I have a Sword
that will not only Cut but likewise Thrust, do one
as well as the other (as in my time I've had several)
I dare under take to answer the bravest Small-Sword
Man in the Universe, by reason I have a double Advantage : In the first Place, I'm upon equal Terms
with him, as to Thrusting; then for Cutting, I
have ten times more odds, for if he Thrusts in Cart
at me, I'll but Strike or Cut at the same time as he
presents his Thrust; and I will lay my Life I can
disable him upon the Wrist, he can no ways evade
it: Otherwise, If he Thrusts again at me, then I'll
Parre him; and in spite of Fate Cut his Arm in his
Recovery. Further, I affirm that there is no Man
living can lie in any Posture whatever at Small-
Sword, but without fail I can cut the Wrist of his
Arm, and no hazard to my self, it is impossible for
any Man to Parre a Stroke or Cut, unless he truly
understood Broad-Sword: What I've said. I think,
is sufficient to convince a rational Man in this Matter, &c.

Now

NOW according to Order, I fhall proceed to Quarter-Staff, the common Length is feven Foot, I divide it into three Parts thus, The Part which you take firft hold on, I call the Handle or Butt end of the Staff, the Middle is half Part of the Staff, the Remainder compleats the Length of the Staff. It is a true *Britifh* Weapon, of great Antiquity, much Practifed and Admired in former Days, to give it its due Praife, 'tis a moft Noble Weapon, and very ufeful in feveral Refpects, 'tis in the Nature of a double Weapon, by reafon when you Exercife it, you make ufe of both Hands. I wonder that it is not more in Vogue in this Nation, confidering its Excellency, for a Man that rightly underftands it, may bid defiance, and laugh at any other Weapon, for it has a double Advantage in many kinds of all others, the long Pike, half Pike, or Pitch-fork, may be term'd Fools to't, nay, they can't in the leaft come in Competition with it. As to the Grounds and Rudiments thereof, foly depends both of Broad and Small-Sword, upon the Broad-Sword, more in refference to the Blows, Chops, Strokes, Slips and Travefes; It only borrows from the Small-Sword the Longe, Thrufts and Darts. No Weapon is learnt or underftood fo foon as this, becaufe there's fo little Variety in it, and the Method fo eafy and plain. Therefore I don't defign to make a long Preamble to a little Matter, but explain the Guards, which are the Infide, Outfide, Medium, and Pendent. You Advance or Raife the Guards on this manner, Stand upon a full or entire Body, fome two Foot fpace with your Legs, and lay your Staff at length upon the Ground, then take hold of the Butt end with your left Hand, advance it middle height, and take hold forward with your right Hand,

Hand, about a Foot diftant from your left; fo bring
the middle of your Staff by your left Ear, round the
back of your Head, ftepping at the fame time with
your right Foot, an equal diftance from the left,
fo you come to an infide Guard; the Butt end of
your Staff then will be againft your left Side, both
your Arms being ftiffly extended, the other Part of
your Staff will crofs your Oppofer's Eyes : Lying on
this manner, if your Oppofer makes a Blow or
Stroke to your left Ear or infide, you are then pre-
pared with a true Guard.   In order to come an outfide, you muft return your Staff by your right Ear,
likewife your Foot into the Place from whence it
came, and you may come to an outfide Guard, the
Butt end of your Staff then will be annenft your right
Side, and the other Part will crofs your Oppofer's
Eyes the contrary way : Lying on this manner, if
your Oppofer ftrikes at your right Ear, you are
then upon a fecure Guard.   From thence you may
come to a Medium, by dropping the Point of your
Staff, and bringing it by your left Ear, and withal
ftep with your right Foot, the fame diftance you did
before, then place it betwixt your Oppofer's Eyes,
this is the Medium Guard : Now if your Oppofer
charge you with a Blow or Stroke at your Head,
Crofs his Staff and 'twill make a perfect Guard. From
the Medium you may come to the Pendent, which I
call the high Guard thus, Slip your right Hand almoft to the left, and return your Staff round the
back of your Head, then your Point will flope or hang
dipping; but obferve that you fee your Oppofer's
Head twelve Inch under the Butt end of your Staff, or
you can in no meafure be fafe   I do not approve of
this Guard, tho' it was in much efteem formerly, but
'tis not valued; the Reafon is, Becaufe the Point of
your Staff being dipt, your Defence is weak: The

in or outside Guard at length, which I call the low Guards, is much the stronger, and far the better.

Imprimis. Admit that you come to exercise with any Man, lie upon a low outside Guard, then if your Opposer strikes at your open on the inside, crosshis Staff, which makes an absolute Guard, and withal the Life and Quickness imaginable, return your Blow to his inside. If you lie upon an outside, when he strikes at your outside, then Guard and Answer quick to the inside. 2*ly.* Come to the outside order again, and if your Opposer strikes at your inside open, Guard and answer with a Dart; that is, make a full and home Thrust with a Longe, like Cart in Ters at Small-Sword, to his outside. 3*ly.* Lie again upon the inside order, and when your Opposer strikes to your outside, Guard and answer with a Dart to his outside: I have been a Professor of the Noble Science above this thirty Years, and I never yet saw the Artist that cou'd defend himself from either of these Darts; but no Man can perform 'em, unless he be a great Proficient in the Art of Small-Sword, because they soly depend upon the true Planting of a Thrust. 4*ly.* Lie again upon the outside, and when your Opposer strikes to the inside, Guard and return your Blow over his Point, to the outside of his right Leg. 5*ly* If you lie again upon the inside, and your Opposer strikes at the outside Guard, then fall your Blow to the inside of his right Leg; there is no ways to escape being hit by either of these Answers, but to withdraw your Leg out of his Distance. 6*ly* A Slip at Staff is perform'd thus; Lie upon an outside, and when your Opposer strikes at you, instead of Guarding, Slip him; that is, withdraw the Butt end of your Staff, as far as your right Ear, and fall back with your Body; then Pitch your Stroke in with a Longe, directly upon a Medium to his Head,

E   and

and you may eafily knock any Man down, fo far
as the Ground will let him fall ; but befure you lapfe
no time in the performance of this Slip, you may
Slip thus from either Infide or Medium.   7*ly.* Engage your Oppofer's Staff ftrongly with your's on
the infide about the middle, prefs his Staff down as
low as his Wafte, then flide your Blow a long the
Staff to his Face : you may perform the like, by engaging your Oppofer's Staff on the outfide, and perform as before directed.   8*ly.* Lie upon a Medium,
and engage the middle of his Staff on the infide, advance one Step, difengage, flide or flip your Hands
together along the Staff, and make your Blow on his
Arm, or right fide of the Head, or put in the Dart.
9*ly.* Engage again on the infide of your Oppofer's
Staff, then flip your Staff as atorefaid, and ftrike full
upon the outfide of his Staff, and fo you may with
great eafe thro' it out of his Hand, then make your
Blow with all Expedition imaginable . you may eafily ftrike a Staff out of any Man's Hand, when you
lie out at length, without fliping your Hands. 10*ly.*
You come up to half Staff, on this manner, Lie upon a Medium, engage your Oppofer's Staff about
the middle, with the end of your's, upon either in
or outfide, advance one ftep, and flip your Hands a
long the Staff, then both ends of your Staff will be
upon a Level, your Hands two Foot diftance from
each other, your Arms extended, holding your Staff
half a Foot higher than your Head, being upon a
full Body, I call this the Level Guard, but I don't
like it . Indeed, if your Oppofer makes a down right
Pitch at you, you are fafe; but if he fhou'd Strike
fliding a long the Staff, 'tis ten to one but he may
difoblige your Knuckles , but to prevent that, Guard
him with one end of your Staff, that is, according
as he makes his Blow, you muft prepare your Guard.
                                                  'T is

'Tis a very nice thing to Play half Staff well, because it depends so much upon the quick slipping of your Hands on the Staff; your cunning in Traveling, (whereby you may gain several Advantages,) and the right putting in of the Dart, which I can't express in Words, but 'tis soon done in Action. Take notice, That the Falsifies at Staff are like to them at Broad-Sword, made over the Point of the Staff; you can make but a single Falsify at Staff, it will not allow doubling on't, by reason you consume so much time in Performance. A Falsify at Staff when you are out of Length with a Step, is a grand Cheat; you may make it in different manner, that is, pretend to Strike on the inside, and conclude on the outside, or pretend to make a Blow on the out, and finish on the inside: You may Falsify after the same manner at half Staff, as you do at Length, without using step. A False Dart at Staff, is a most excellent thing, and very dangerous to the Opposer, it is perform'd after the same way as a Feint at Small-Sword, with a Longe, either to your In, or Outside; and if you chance or design'dly hit your Opposer in the Face, with a Dart or Thrust, 'tis much odds you'l Eclipse one of his Eyes : You now find that Quarter-Staff hath its dependance both of Broad and Small-Sword, as I have explain'd before, &c.

Concise Rules at Wrestling, plainly demonstrated.

1*st*. THE Holds that are taken, are commonly call'd, dignified or distinguish'd by Lose or Fast, out or in Holds, thus explain'd, Lose is perform'd on this manner, viz. Approach to your Opposer upon an entire Body, and when you are within Distance, that is, two Foot from him; withal the Quicknefs imaginable, Trip or Strike with your right Foot the back of his left, and at the fame juncture as your right Foot hit his, let the Palm of your Hand fall forceably upon his Breaft; fo Hand and Foot being timed together, you may make it a clear fall.   The out Holds are taken thus, Seize or take Hold of the Parties right Elbow with your left Hand, then with your right Hand take faft hold on his left Shoulder, and immediately twift or bring him withal the Strength and Force you have, ftriking at the fame time, if you pleafe, with your right Foot the outfide his left Ham, and you may thro' or caft him towards your right Side.   Otherways, Take hold on the Parties right Elbow as aforefaid, then put your right Arm over his left Shoulder, and take faft hold on his Back with your right Hand, about the height of his Wafte, hold faft your holds, ftand about two Foot diftant with your Legs, in this Capacity you may clofe a Lock, call'd, The In'turn; that is, put your right Leg the infide his left, and clap the Lock in the Ham of his left Leg, fecure faft your Holds, and you may thro' or caft the Party backward, by winding your Body clofe to his, and fall with him, ftill holding your Holds with your Hands, and lofe the Lock you have taken in his Ham, then put your Leg up his Grainnens, fo wind or bring him forward.   From thence you may come to a Crofs-Buttock, that is, continue the Holds that you have taken with your Hands, and place your right Leg equally betwixt his, then wind your Buttock under his Belly, bend or incline your Head forward, raife him from the Ground, hit the outfide of his right Ancle with the Heel of your right Foot, and you may make a fore Fall.   2ly. If you wou'd take another over or out Hold, fecure the right Elbow with your left Hand as aforefaid, then put

your

your right Arm over his right Shoulder, and take
fast hold on his Wafte with your right Hand, about
the middle of his Back, then clafp or take the Lock
with your right Leg in the Ham of his right, wind
your Body forward, and you may caft or thro' the
Party backward : From this Hold you may take the
In'turn upon his left Leg, and thro' him backward,
ftill fecuring your Holds with your Hands, and by
lofing the Lock, you may come to a Crofs-Buttock,
that is, wind your Buttock under his Belly, in like
manner as aforefaid, and thro' him in manner as a-
forefaid. 3*ly*. Another out Hold is taken thus, Seize
upon the Wrift of your Oppofer's right Arm with
your right Hand, keep his Arm upon the ftretch or
extendedly, then clap your left Shoulder under the
Elbow of his right Arm, and caft or thro' the Party
over your Head, by this means you may eafily break
his Arm. Or thus, Seize the Wrift of his left Arm
with your left Hand, and clap your right Shoulder
under the Elbow of his left Arm, and Pitch him likewife over your Head, by either of thefe Ways, you
may, with great eafe, break any Man's Arm; for
'tis moral impoffible, any Perfons Arm fhou'd bear
the weight of his Body without breaking. 4*ly*. To
take an in Hold or under Hold, which is all one,
fecure the right Elbow as aforefaid, then clap your
right Hand upon his left Side, and by degrees, or
with what Expedition you can, move it three Parts
round his Waft, then clap the Point of your right
Shoulder annenft his left Breaft, and that preferves
you from being lifted, in this Order you may come
to feveral Holds, *viz* The In'turn backward and
forward, and perform as aforefaid : Or thus, Lofe
the Lock, and hold faft your Hands, and place your
right Leg equally betwixt his, then you may come
to the Crofs-Buttock, which is taken with greater

eafe

eafe by an in Hold than an out, perform'd as aforefaid ; which being exquifitly done, it's the foreft Fall
that can be thrown : Securing ftill your Holds with
your Hands, you may come to a Lock, I call the
Hitch, that is, put your right Leg betwixt his, and
clap the Heel of your Foot on the back of the Ancle
of his right Leg, then poife or prefs him backward ;
ftill fecuring the right Elbow, you may come to a
back Lock thus, Clap your right Foot upon the outfide his left, fo that your Toe will be againft his
Heel, then lock the Knee, by keeping your right
Foot in its place, and putting your Knee the in Side
his, fo you may eafily thro' him backward over
your Knee ; ftill fecuring the right Elbow, then clap
your right Leg level upon the bottom of his Belly,
and you may Lock upon his left Thigh with your
right Foot, the right Arm over his left Shoulder,
holding faft on his Neck, and if he raifes you from
the Ground, continue your Holds, and when he fets
you down, then you may Crofs-Buttock him in like
manner as aforefaid ; this dexteroufly perform'd,
will puzzle a good Gamfter to avoid being thrown,
The next Hold that you may take, is call'd the Cornifh Hug, which may be taken with the one Arm
under, the other over, but both Arms under is the
beft and eafieft way, thus, L'ofe the Hold that you've
taken on the Parties right Elbow, and with both
your Arms quite environe, his Waft being faft gript
about him, Hug or clofe him faft to your Breaft,
lean a little back with your Body, raife him from
the Ground, and caft or thro' him over your right
or left Thigh, which you find beft for your Advantage ; I do really believe, the *Cornifh* Men perform's
this Hold the beft of any Men in Chriftendom, we
borrow it from thence.   Another curious Hold may
be taken thus, Take faft Hold on the Parties Wrift

of his right Hand with your left, then quicker than I can fpeak, clap your right Shoulder under his right Arm-pit, fink a little with your Body, and clap your right Hand upon his Back to hold him clofe to you, then raife him from the Ground, and thro' him over your Head; this, if truly perform'd, may be made the worft Fall that can be thrown, I call this the Flying Mare; Still fecure your Hold that you've taken on his Wrift, put your right Arm under his right, and half encompafs his Waft with it, then clap your right Thigh the outfide his left Ham, fo bring or caft him backward over your right Thigh.

I have known fome Men fo ftupidly vain glorious, and felf conceited of their Abilities, as to fay, they will give a Man leave to take hold where'er he pleafes, yet lay any Wager they can thro' him : To convince their Ignorance, take this Method, Let him ftand upon a full Body, ftep behind him, and put both your Arms betwixt his Legs, then let him ftoop or bend with his Body forward, fo low that you can take hold of the Wrifts of both his Hands with your's, hold faft your Holds, and you are fecure from being thrown your felf, but its the Devil to a Bodle, you may Pitch him upon his Head. I fhall hint another fubtil Piece of Art, and fo conclude, Whereas, I'm to take what Hold or Holds I pleafe, to my beft Advantage, Let a Man ftand as aforefaid, ftep behind him, then extend both your Arms, and put them under his Arm-pits; he muft ftoop fome what low with his Head to give Advantage; then you muft take faft hold upon the back of his Neck, with both your Fingers gript one within another, by that means you may fix him in a pretty becoming Pofture, vulgarly call'd the Pilloiy.

The

The most excellent way or manner of breaking Holds that can be taken of you.

IMprimis, If your Oppofer takes an In'turn of you, fpring the Lock, that is, keep your Leg, that which he takes the Lock upon, faft on the Ground, your Foot being turn'd a little outward, then ftiffen ftarken, or ftretch your Ham ftiff, by a fudden fpring, and 'twill break the Lock; then raife him from the Ground, and caft him from you, in manner of a *Cornifh* Hug; all In'turns may be broken fo. The Crofs-Buttock is broken by turning your Buttock to the Parties you are engaged with, and quitting your Holds; or rather thus, When your Oppofer doth Crofs-Buttock you, before he has raifed you from the Ground, (before to time that) clap the Edge of your Hand very hard under his Chin, or the Palm of your Hand upon his Nofe, thefe ways breaks all Holds that can be taken. How to difengage from the Holds taken of your Collar, If your Oppofer takes hold on your Collar, with his left Hand, and keeps you ftiffly out at length, then feize faft hold with your left Hand, on the upper part of his Wrift, then twift or turn his Wrift inward with your full Strength, and at the fame juncture Strike forceably upon the Elbow of his Arm, which will much endanger to break it · If the Party fhould take hold of your Collar with his right Hand, then lay hold of his Wrift with your right Hand, and perform as aforefaid, *&c.*

F I N I S.

Milton Keynes UK
Ingram Content Group UK Ltd.
UKHW022219121023
430490UK00005B/182